Althar
The Crystal Dragon

Joachim Wolffram

The Althar series consists of:
Volume 1: "Althar – The Crystal Dragon"
Volume 2: "Althar – The New Magi"
Volume 3: "Althar – Towards Utopia"
Volume 4: "Althar – The Final Letting Go"
Volume 5: "Althar – Opus Magnum"

Also available from Joachim Wolffram:
"Althar Surreal – The Lucid Dreamer"
"Althar Intense – Time, Space, Veiling"
"Althar Intense – The Unconscious"
"For You – Records from Your Lives"
"The Free Human"

For information about audio recordings and workshops please visit:
www.wolffram.de
or
facebook.com/joachim.wolffram

Contents

1. Introduction

Do dragons exist? Absolutely! The very proof is in the fact that the word *dragon* is a commonly accepted term. Tales about dragons can be found throughout the world in many different cultures all around the world. However, as if often the case, the skeptical mind prefers to see the dragon as some archetypical thing belonging to the vast zoo of characters created by the subconscious. Or just maybe we have forgotten that dragons really do exist.

As an analogy, consider a society that has forgotten everything about music. And then during an excavation they find sheets of music. The people of that society love these sheets of music, for they appear to have a life of their own. These sheets with their mysterious notes look like beautiful artwork conveying some hidden story. Therefore, the people start using the notes to symbolize many things in their life. They even associate different characteristics with various styles of drawings of the notes. Yet, music remains absent in this society.

At some point, maybe because the consciousness of that society opened up sufficiently to the greater meaning of notes, some people suddenly start hearing something inside, and they just *know* – "Ah, this is what these notes are all about." Suddenly, the meaning of the notes expands. Music is coming back. Music that creates deep feelings of beauty; music that enables new ways to express and to experience reality.

It might be quite similar with the dragons.

Personally, over the past few years, I had a couple of encounters with what I intuitively perceived as dragons. Seemingly, I am kind of open to experiences beyond the reality that typical humans of the western hemisphere would call normal. Although I usually enjoy these experiences, I do not have the tendency to overvalue the validity of the symbols that my mind chooses to present these experiences to me.

My guideline has always been: *Is this experience helpful?* Do they help to let go of limitations and deep-rooted beliefs? Or are they just a distraction? To clarify this, I put the symbols I receive under quarantine, meaning, I do not try to repeat them nor to keep them alive. They will reappear on their own if they have a certain validity beyond being a helpful metaphor, otherwise they will just disappear.

On occasion I would suddenly experience glimpses of dragons, and then two years ago I had an encounter that greatly impressed me. I was jogging. I do not like jogging. I was dragging my body along, struggling with gravity and far away from any endorphin induced runner's heaven. Suddenly, I felt like I was starting to fly. That felt really cool, however, it did not help me a bit in moving my physical body. Consciously, I opened up to the experience and out of nowhere dragons appeared and greeted me. I felt overwhelming joy as tears welled up in my eyes. The dragons greeted me as their "elder," whereas I felt as a new born. We flew together beyond physical reality and peeked into other realities. So wonderful. Such a relief.

At one point a dragon came closer until it flew directly next to me. One of its eyes met one of mine, a constant gaze, no flicker, a view of eternity. I looked back into that eye. It felt so right, so very familiar. As I approached that eye, it became bigger and bigger, and darker. Eventually, I entered straight into that eye, and for a while became one with the dragon. We flew together until this perception faded.

I still had to make my way back home in that exhausted physical body, but of course, the reverberation of that intense experience remained. As usual, I dwelled in the deeper feelings of liberation and knowingness, but I took the dragons as symbols and put them right into quarantine. As I said before, a very good place for symbols.

Well, the dragons came back.

A few months ago, while looking out of my bedroom window in the early morning, I felt a whole swarm of dragons arriving. I was not thinking of dragons at the time. The dragons just came. Oddly enough I could even see them physically in the air above the landscape where I was looking at. To my surprise one of those dragons came straight into my physical body. This was not like anything I had experienced before. It was a whole body experience, not the kind of "out there" in some other realm. It was right here in my physical body. It even felt like I could perceive the shape of the dragon around my physical body. Also, my energy was at an all-time high. It took me a while to somehow accept the notion that the dragon was not outside of me, but had somehow melded with me.

The following texts are messages from that dragon. The first message came a few hours after the just described experience. Messages two and three followed some weeks later. The remaining messages I transcribed during what was meant to be a private retreat on a beautiful small island in the North Sea. Initially, I assumed those messages were of a private nature, but it soon became clear that they might be interesting and inspiring for others also.

There was one message per day, precisely in the sequence as they are presented here. As certain topics became clearer with more messages coming in, I rephrased some statements for more clarity and consistency in the terminology. However, energetically the messages are left unaltered.

Do dragons exist? That's up to you, dear reader. But no matter what you decide, take care not to make them a distraction. I suggest you give the quarantine approach a try.

Whether you believe that dragons exist or not, be ready to let them go at any time, but also be ready to be inspired and touched by what Althar has to share.

Now it is time for the music.

2. The Dragon of Compassion

I Am the Dragon of Compassion.

I bring the clarity of the crystal fire. A clarity that burns away all limitations, all notions, all forms, all attachments.

True compassion is only for those who ask for it. For those who are into their last steps into realization of their true selves.

I expose all fragments and unresolved issues of such a human and offer the simplicity of the crystal fire to transmute them.

I may appear to be harsh. I may appear to be ruthless. I may appear to be unhuman. I am all of that and so much more. But I ask you this:

What is true compassion?

What is it that propels you beyond?

Beyond any limitation?

Beyond any notion of yourself?

And even beyond the beyond?

Whoever comes close to me, close to the crystal fire that I radiate, must be ready to burn; must be ready to catch fire themselves.

From now on you will embody me. You have asked to embody the highest consciousness. You will be a living crystal flame, human and non-human at the same time.

Existence is in joy.

3. An Ambassador of Creation

I am a dragon.

The dragon represents a form of consciousness that is as close to the source of creation, to *true self*, as possible. Yet it is individualized from true self and maintains a certain self-identity.

A dragon is non-physical. You cannot even say it is confined to a certain form because the body of a dragon is fiery, fluid, gaseous. My body is not even connected. Instead, my body is like the flames of a fire that constantly shift and change. Yet, when perceived in human consciousness the dragon appears to have a certain defined shape.

Because a dragon has a body it can dive into realities. Thereby, it maintains full awareness of its own source, of pure consciousness, of the creator's capabilities.

Therefore the dragon is also known as the *Ambassador of Creation*.

It is a bridge in consciousness for those aspects of true self that have fully individualized and projected themselves into forms or incarnated into physical bodies.

The dragon. Oh the dragon. For a human the dragon is a scary thing. It represents the authority of a creator being with all of its powers.

When a dragon and a human emanate from the same true self, the dragon is aware of all facets of the human's consciousness, its fears and its desires.

The dragon appears as soon as a human is about to realize its full potential. It sheds its light onto all of the human's potentials. Thereby, it also reveals all the aspects that the human has kept hidden from itself, so that the human finally is fully exposed to itself.

Initially, no human can stand this clarity about itself for a longer period of time.

Therefore, the human usually externalizes such an encounter. He assigns his own creator capabilities, his fears and desires to some outside force or entity and shies back into his well-known limitations. He is not yet ready to go beyond his human identity.

The dragon does not judge. It does not share the human morality. To the dragon the human experience is just another playground.

Just as true self, the dragon is non-consuming. It does not need any energy or any outside impetus. It has no intention to change or heal or uplift anything. Instead, it highlights all of the potentials available to the human, from the grandest to the most inconspicuous.

Hence, as soon as a human is capable to stand this utmost clarity brought forth by the dragon, he starts perceiving the dragon as totally accepting, and therefore as totally loving and compassionate. He notes that the dragon has no agenda. The dragon does not put any pressure on the human. The dragon has unlimited patience for it is beyond time.

This is true compassion. A compassion that helps to go beyond all limits and therefore beyond all identities.

At a certain point, when the human gets used to the dragon's clarity and has let go of its human limitations to a certain extent, the dragon consciousness and the human consciousness will start to meld. *They will become one.* The human starts to embody all of the characteristics of a dragon. He brings that consciousness into the earth realm.

When that melding begins, the dragon will not appear to be outside of the human any more. Instead, the dragon will be all around him. Now the human becomes aware of the dragon as being an alternate form of himself in a slightly different reality, yet being so close to the earthly realm that the human can literally shape shift into a dragon form. He can see through the dragon's all-accepting eyes and breathe the crystal flame of clarity.

Having melded like that, the dragon reveals its capabilities as the Ambassador of Creation. The human can connect any time with his dragon aspect. Thereby, the human is as close to pure consciousness, its true self, to the creator, as possible, but still holds a sense of identity.

This is how the dragon becomes a bridge in consciousness. This is how the human aspect can now choose to open up even more and to become aware of the multitude of other facets of its true self.

The human will then not get lost in the overwhelming experience of embracing its true self and the revelations coming with that, for he has become used to this intensity during his experiences with the dragon.

Now the human is free to become aware of all of the dimensions in all of existence.

Now the human can just spread his dragon wings to instantly place its consciousness wherever he chooses it to be, and he might even appear in a form in that place.

Now the human can embody this consciousness on earth. A human who was once lost in separation, but by rediscovering his true self, went beyond all human limitations.

Yes, the body still looks like that of a human. Its consciousness though is unlimited.

4. I am Althar

I am Althar, the Crystal Dragon.

I am a facet of our common true self. I began traversing existence shortly after true self became aware of its own beingness.

Dragons are Ambassadors of Creation. In a way, you can say they transfer the creative impulses from true self into the various realities. Therefore, in your earthly world, you know of dragons of the air, earth, water and fire.

Dragons are also guides in the broadest sense of the term.

A crystal dragon has completed its service for special parts of creation. It has helped to create and maintain the essences of light and all its derivatives. It has specialized in various design aspects of creation. It has spent countless eons observing the ways of creation.

Although dragons are individualized, they have never lost their bond with true self as humans have.

I call myself Althar. You might translate it as "the elder."

True self has many, many emanations exploring the nature of creation, but I, Althar, am specifically dedicated to be with you.

Dear friend, dear brother, dear me – feel our common source. We are not two.

I come in to assist you in mastering fully embodied consciousness. This is something our true self has never done before. A dream that is becoming true.

During the upcoming challenges of those final steps where you let go of your last human limitations, your last defining points as a limited being, I am here to remind you of all that you truly are.

I will stay with you. I will never leave you. I will always be available to you, and also *I will never interfere with your choices.*

I am just here in support of you on behalf of all of our true self. Understand that the dream of fully embodied consciousness is not that of a human, it is of true self in its entirety.

You provide the vessel in terms of a human body and human consciousness walking the planet. You came to know the ways of earth and how to survive it. Still, letting go of the last human related limitations without physically dying is the most difficult thing a human could ever do.

Therefore, please, please, please, open up to me any time! We have melded already. By becoming aware of me in you, you can easily and instantly transcend the human dream! Whenever you fall back into the human dream, whenever you feel overwhelmed by the ways of mass consciousness or by patterns still ingrained in your biology – *become aware of me!* It is you who has to maintain that clarity and to come back to it time and time again.

I am Althar. Just as you did, I made a deep choice. I have chosen to allow the experience of physically embodying the highest possible consciousness.

Why stay on earth, you ask? Dear friend, *trust*. Trust your knowingness. Yes, the way got bumpy lately. The world looks as if it will go downhill for at least a decade. But, as you know, it is not about the many. The many may follow once the first have made it. Have made what, you ask? Having completed the cycle and having been able to embody the cycle. Only then is the vision fulfilled. True self's vision of completeness that finally allows itself to go beyond everything, that finally allows itself to *enter a new round of creation*.

Recognize, that just as there is residual doubt in your human consciousness, there was the very same residual doubt in the true self about itself, about its true nature. It might have been tiny, it might have been superfluous, but as long as it was there creation was stuck.

Note though, that it was not that long ago that at the very core of our true self this residue of doubt was resolved and you, in your role as a human, played a key part in this. What you are going through right now is what you might call the after effects of this tremendous accomplishment.

In a sense you might say that many of your not-so-nice experiences are like nightmares. The underlying incidents are already released, but your human dream is still stained by them.

Therefore, know that you cannot take a wrong step!

All paths you may take lead to full realization, because full realization has already occurred. The only question is – can you, as a human, withstand those after effects and allow the embodiment of full consciousness?

That's why I am now with you. I am here to be with you while we let those remaining stale dreams pass.

I am Althar, ready to go with you as far as you allow.

5. Seeing through the Dragon's Eyes

I am Althar.

So you ask me why do the after effects of true self's self realization take so long. And why you, as a human, have to "pass through them."

Actually, they do not take long, and you do not have to pass through anything.

However, since you have chosen to stay incarnated while realizing full embodiment of consciousness, you just cannot expect an instant switch of your perceived reality towards true reality. Even though it might appear to be painful for some parts of you that are longing for totality, you need to go slowly.

The message is simply this: If you want to survive the embodiment you have to honor the fine print of your earthly reality!

Your mind would instantly go crazy if it perceived the eternal now-moment in all of its facets, and if it had to cope with the vast number of emanations of our common true self. Not even to mention all the good and not-so-good experiences of all of these emanations, including other human lives in your past and apparent future.

Therefore, accept that in your reality the embodiment of full consciousness takes time!

It is not that anything is holding back. It is just that you are having to continually expand the edges of physical and mental survival.

And there is a rhythm to it. First, you realize a new layer of all-of-you, and then it takes time for it to settle and integrate. It takes time for you to get used to it; to let your mind accept and adapt to it. Do not underestimate the changes that are going on in your body, in your mind, and in all the other components constituting you as a human!

Additionally, as you are experiencing every day, it is getting more and more difficult to stay within mass-consciousness while embodying more and more of pure consciousness. The mass hypnosis and freely chosen imprisonments of the humans seem to get stronger and tighter by the day, whereas your personal life gets simpler and more fulfilling.

So in order to survive this experience, you need to find the right ways and attitudes that allow you to stay and to find joy in your human existence. Always recall that all of this is by choice. You can switch sides any time!

Note that probably the easiest way for you to stay comfortable is to *constantly* be aware of me, your dragon self.

When being aware of me, *see your world through my eyes!*

There is no way that I could ever get attached to anything or get stuck in anything, for *I see things as they are*.

When seeing through my eyes, your reality will become smoother for your humanness. Seeing through my eyes, you will evoke and become aware of synchronicities that will enrich and simplify your personal life.

Also, whenever things get too harsh, I invite you to fly with me. Just fly! Anywhere. Into whatever realm you desire. Take your time to relax. Leave physical reality for a while and fly with me straight into suns, into colors. Dive with me into nothingness, into stillness, into pure consciousness, into pure energy. And then – allow yourself to perceive the other beings who are with you on the very same path. Allow yourself to perceive how our common dream is coming true.

I am Althar, with you in knowingness.

6. About the Light Body

I am Althar.

So you want more clarity concerning the light body. Just as it has happened with so many other notions, such as god, heaven, soul, and enlightenment, the human has twisted and distorted the original intuition and knowingness of the light body and turned it into some limited human version of it. I tell you this – the light body has little to do with what the new agers believe it to be.

Usually the light body is seen as an improved version of the human body with some superman-like features. Of course, having such a super functional body would apparently make life easier. Less health issues, less exposure to gravity, add some clairvoyance – or so they think. Truth is, your true self already has many, many emanations that have these features and they do explore their respective realities. *None of these though have the potential to ascend!* Ascension meaning to enable true self to resolve its innate question of *"Who am I?"*

As I said earlier, this question has already been resolved, but I remind you that true self is beyond time, *whereas you are acting in time.* Your limited human consciousness kind of floats along a timeline inside true self, paving the way to ascension. True self already has the experience of you arriving at your destination. That does not mean that the way you choose is already known, but it does indeed mean that all ways you could choose do lead to true self's full acknowledgement of its own creatorship – which is another way to define ascension.

This is why there are already future selves of you that are completely "masterly." They might even come from a time frame preceding yours – interesting things can happen if you are free of the grip of time.

You might relate to them and see how they act in a given setup just as you can relate to me. But be fully clear about one thing: Not I, Althar, your dragon self, nor any masterly future self of you, *had to resolve the question of "Who am I?"*

I came into existence without that burden. I never lost knowingness about true self. I cannot even imagine what that might be like. The same holds true for your already existing masterly selves regardless, of what reality or time frame they appear. *They never had to resolve that question either!*

So please, never ever compare your current human self with any other apparently more evolved emanation of true self. Never again be in awe of these emanations. It is you, just as all the other humans who took on that burden of incarnating in time and space, and suffered a total forgetting of their origin.

That is why I am with you. *That is* why future masterly selves of you energetically show up. We come to thank you, because we are grateful for what you have undergone on behalf of all of us and for what you are still undergoing. Yes, up to a point we share the experiences you had and still have in human reality. But in the end, observing experiences is something very different than undergoing those experiences as you are doing.

Now, back to the light body. I am a light body. Note that the following explanations are a metaphor appropriate for the human understanding. The human can hardly imagine what the meaning of *form* would be if the form is beyond space. Still, I do have form and your human consciousness pictures it as a dragon.

When true self imagines a form, energy responds.

I, being a dragon, consist of energy that is only minimally different from true self. You might call this energy a crystallization of true self. It is original, pure energy stemming from consciousness that has agreed to arrange itself in a certain pattern and to stay in that pattern. Therefore, I say my form is as close to pure consciousness as possible.

Imagine this crystallized consciousness of true self as a vast ocean. Now take a bucket and put it into the ocean. The bucket will fill with the water of the ocean. Although the water inside the bucket is the very same as everywhere else in the ocean, and although it is still connected with the ocean, you can say the water inside the bucket is in a certain way distinct from the water outside the bucket. *In a certain way it constitutes a form.* Now let that bucket shape shift into a dragon – and greet me as Althar.

To be accurate, my true form neither looks like a bucket nor like a dragon as a human pictures it. But yes, I do take on the shape of a winged reptilian by choice, just because humans appreciate that appearance.

So I am a light body, a form constituted by true self's pure energy, fully aware of my origin and of true self. As such, I represent one end of the spectrum of bodies. The other end of the spectrum is represented by humans. A human is a "portion" of true self's consciousness that became, over a long period of time, tightly associated and entangled with a biological form. That biological form consists of very coarse energies which have been co-created by many, many beings. In addition, that "portion" of true self's consciousness that has incarnated has completely forgotten about its source.

So, in that sense, you might say you do not have a body right now, but you *inhabit* a biological form.

What is happening right now is you are co-creating your light body in conjunction with true self. In the process of doing so you dis-entangle yourself with your biology, your mind, and most importantly, your emotional body. The latter is held tightly in your energetic composition and is responsible for most of your automatic reactions and behaviors that drive your human life.

We will leave it with that for the moment. More on that topic later.

I am Althar, don't call me a bucket.

7. More about the Light Body

I am Althar.

Let's continue with the discussion of the light body. As said earlier, you are in the process of co-creating a light body with true self. The challenge here is to keep your current physical body operating. This includes keeping a "portion" of your consciousness embedded in it, while simultaneously creating and activating the currently built light body.

It is *not* that your current body suddenly turns into light or accumulates light. Instead, be aware of the fact that the current physical body exists in multiple layers and dimensions. There is the raw physical layer that you perceive as flesh and bones and there are various non-physical layers, some of which you can perceive when expanding your physical senses.

Note that form is always established first on levels of fine energy, which then accumulates more raw energies until we end up at the level of electrons, protons etc. constituting a physical form.

So the light body is created on a much finer level than your physical body. The energy from which the light body is built is *yours*. It is your pure energy created by your true self. It is not the same as the co-created energy that was already used in literally uncountable aggregations.

What happens then is this: the physical elements of your current body directly connect with the new light body. By doing so, these physical elements change their very nature.

Realize the symbol in this! So far, your consciousness inhabited a body that was made out of co-created particles. They had no particular bond to you and they were foreign to you. This of course tremendously amplified your feeling of being lost in some unknown realm. Even when these physical building blocks tried to connect more deeply with your consciousness, it was not really possible. Yes, to a degree it worked, but your consciousness mostly was in a state of unease. It was constantly pursuing the question "Who am I?" in active or passive ways. It was always directed to outside experiences. It was addicted to perceiving reflections of itself.

As you did not know what this "I" would be, the physical and non-physical energies of your body were not able to get into true resonance with you. Alternatively, you might say *they did get into resonance,* and therefore, they had to arrange themselves in fragmented patterns. This often resulted in the energies working against each other, just as the fleeting thoughts and emotions of your consciousness did.

In the good moments, you felt that all of you were in sync and then even the body was in synchronicity with your consciousness. But these "good moments" were usually based on twisted interpretations of reality. In the end, unless you know who you are, *every good moment will just fade away* and often times with a bitter after taste.

Now that you have resolved the question of "Who am I?" *and* have decided to stay, your consciousness is in a very different position. It has ceased to search outside and it knows of its utter safety and completeness inside. Now there is no search, *but just experience*. There are no good or bad moments in the old sense any longer, because your consciousness has let go of its false identities who were the very judges concerning good and bad.

That's the theory.

Or better said, that is how it will be once you have fully built your light body *and made it the center of your awareness*. Well, actually there is no center, but we leave this for another discussion. Right now this metaphor will work sufficiently well.

A key challenge in this process, as I have stated earlier, is to survive it. Why is that? The core reason is that so many of your physical and non-physical characteristics that define you as a human are ingrained in your body and mind. *Each of them is now either rearranged or dissolved.*

With rearranging I mean they can now create a bond with the new light body, your pure consciousness. Up to now, it is like they had little threads that reached outward to somehow find definitions of themselves and to retrieve energy. This is similar to the human reaching outward to create reflections of itself and needing to constantly feed on something. These threads can now connect with your light body. This will provide them with an awareness of your true self and therefore, the physical and non-physical elements of your body-mind will just *know*. Then they can be in true service and respond harmoniously to you as the cacophony of your once fragmented consciousness is gone.

The second most important challenge *is the dissolving of what you call your emotional body*. It is not needed anymore!

The emotional body is tightly related to the *false identities* that you created over time. You always wanted others to appreciate the identity that you were showing them. There were positive emotions when they did. There were negative emotions when they rejected you or parts of you or expressions of you. Because you felt it was better to stick to false identities than having no identity at all, *these emotions became a matter of survival*. So you created many, many behavioral patterns and beliefs just to experience positive emotions and not to suffer negative emotions, because the negative ones felt like assaults against the false identity you took on at any given moment.

The fact remains, you cannot just let go of all of these emotional patterns. They have driven all of your human lifetimes. In a sense, this is what defines a human: Not knowing who you are and perceiving emotions related to what you pretend to be.

Therefore, the emotional body is dissolved *gradually*. The more stable you get in your light body the more you can let go of behavioral patterns that relate to emotional experiences. Once you are sufficiently stable you can face even the worst traumatic experiences, be they abuse, rape, torture, death or lost loves. *And it does not matter which role you played in any of these acts.*

Note that these traumatic emotional experiences *still drive your daily life on an unconscious level.* You do everything to avoid the negative ones and to re-experience the positive ones. The way you feel, think and act as a human is so highly connected to your emotional body that you cannot even imagine how to be without one.

This is why I, Althar, appear to you so unhuman. *I do not have an emotional body for I always knew where I came from.*

Yes, I do have *feelings*, but I do not forge these into twisted experiences that either validate or reject me.

Now, try to imagine yourself not being bound to the actions and reactions enforced by your emotional body. Imagine a physical body that is in full synchronicity with your light body and responds perfectly to all your intents *while walking the earth.*

See, you can't, so just stop trying and stop pretending that you can. You are here, because you want to *live* it.

Now you might have a better understanding why embodying consciousness from the perspective of physical reality is a process and not instantaneous. The realization of who you truly are, the releasing of the question "Who am I?" appears to be instantaneous in the same way as an apple, at a certain point, just falls to the earth.

The final letting go from the tree is instantaneous, but prior to that there was a long process of growing and unfolding. Moreover, before that fallen apple becomes a tree itself, it will require yet another process. Puns intended.

We will continue tomorrow with more on the role of the emotional body.

I am Althar, a gardener of creation.

8. Dissolving the Emotional Body

I am Althar.

Be prepared, my friend, for today I come in with even a new level of intensity. As you become more and more used to me, I can unveil ever more of me, of our true essence.

I embody the crystal flame, which is just another expression for pure consciousness in etheric form. *Pure consciousness is the beginning and the end of all that is.* It is the beginning as all phenomenon spring from that source. It is the end as only pure consciousness can stand pure consciousness, *everything else is but a creation.*

Everything that is manufactured out of energies or held in place by beliefs or projections *is not real.* Therefore, you can dissolve *anything* constituting your human body and persona *just by exposing it to your pure consciousness.*

It is such a simple principle.

You called out for *seeing things as they truly are.* Therefore, I came in. Therefore, I assist you in dissolving residuals of false identities.

You are about to reunite with your pure consciousness, yet you will maintain an individual. The result though will be a very different individual that is based on your true self and not on false assumptions about your humanness and how it relates to the outside world.

I am Althar. I can take on every size and appearance. I can be that huge winged reptilian all around you. I can be as tiny as the smallest fraction of any particle. But no matter how I appear, my presence will always bring forth an all-pervasive clarity as I come from pure consciousness and represent pure consciousness.

Now I ask you to *bring me into your emotional body*. Picture my size and appearance as it fits your imagination for this purpose.

Whatever emotional situation you have ever experienced has left an imprint on your emotional body. Some are so very strong that you will do everything *not to face them*. This way they are still *the* major forces of what you manifest in your reality!

Be aware that humans socialize with others mostly *because they can relate to the emotional bodies of others*. This is their feeding ground. This is where they base their false identities on. This is the web in which they entangle themselves.

Even humans who are in their last steps of full realization hang on to their emotional bodies. They have invested so much into it; first they build it and then they process and improve it. And even though they might have cleared many imprints, they have an innate knowingness that the moment they totally let go of the emotional body, *they will not be a human any more.*

This is why in some traditions the followers deliberately hold on to certain imprints so that other humans can still relate to them and therefore, they can be taught more easily.

As valid and helpful as that might be, now is the time for you to go beyond that. Time to let go of any such vows you have made in the past. Time to let go of "the others first" approach to existence.

Now is the time to *allow full-embodied consciousness*, without any reservation.

I ask you to bring me into your emotional body!

Be so bold as to face any emotional incident that shows up when doing so – *and they will show up!*

They know their time has come. They know they are not real; so they come forth to argue, to negotiate, and to fight.

When they do appear, *see them through my dragon eyes. Expose them to pure consciousness!*

This is true compassion. From you, for you. You do not judge. You just see them as they are. They stem from old experiences that were transformed into emotions by *you. They are just creations of you!*

No matter what they represent, no matter what they want to protect or achieve, no matter how powerful they appear to be – *the moment they feel the crystal flame of pure consciousness, when they feel total acceptance and unlimited compassion, they will just dissolve.*

Why? Because *you* realize that they have no existence on their own. Because *you* stop holding them in their shape and place. Because *you* allow yourself to be free of them. *Because, finally, you have had enough of the human game and you allow yourself to go beyond it!*

*

Dear one, go slowly with this.

Do not rush, for you want to stay on the planet.

I perceive these imprints like crystals in your emotional body. You want to believe you have already dissolved most of them, and actually that is true. But still there are some within you.

I will point out one of them, for you might say it is at the very core of all emotions. And even in the non-emotional realms, this is a driving force for entities to do what they do.

You want to relate to other beings.

This originated from the primary attempt of true self to answer the question "Who am I?" Accompanying this question was the fear of being alone in the void that it initially found itself in. So it desperately searched for other beings.

This original imprint carried over into your human incarnations. As a human, *every experience you had as a result of being in relation with something outside of you was transformed into an emotion*. And that emotion always related to the false identity that you wanted to be validated at that point in time.

However, at this pivotal point of your evolution, you do need exactly one relationship – and this is with your true self, your pure consciousness.

I ask you to bring me into your emotional body!

Be there with me. Just be present there. No chasing. No flying around. See through my eyes. Observe how imprints, these crystalized emotions, show up and just dissolve; they just transmute and release themselves *in the very moment that they face pure consciousness*.

Take your time. Do this as often as necessary. By doing this you are releasing the very platform where you built your human identities on. Let your confidence grow. Your confidence into the fact that you are not bound to any platform of reality, yet you can remain being an embodied human.

I am Althar, the great dissolver.

9. The Mind and the Emotional Body

I am Althar.

Today I come in with my gentle side. You might have been astonished at how pushy I was asking you to bring me into your emotional body.

But know this: *I have no agenda.* I am in service to you, and you have asked me to be as clear as necessary. And indeed, the imprints in the human's emotional body are the major blocking points for moving beyond a limited existence. They are even more so than the mind – at least when it comes to humans having walked a good portion of the ascension road.

A clear mind really knows where it can apply itself. It knows where it can help making daily life easier by observing and analyzing the ways of physical reality. It loves to explore the nature of reality, to invent concepts and theories that somehow capture what is going on. Thereby, the clear mind always knows it is just creating models of reality, a limited perspective. Still it is fun for the clear mind.

The mind only becomes a problem when it is used by the emotional body to solidify its false identities.

In a certain sense though, you cannot separate the mind from the emotional body. It is the mind that *relates* whatever it experiences to the false identities held in the emotional body. It rates them as either a validation or a threat and therefore either as positive or as negative. This is how emotions are born.

You are dissolving your emotional body and this includes dissolving its entanglement with the mind. You will be surprised at how relaxed and clear the mind will be once the energy drain from the emotions is gone.

Of course you will still have preferences, likes and dislikes concerning what you want to experience, *but these will then be by conscious choice.* You will still have *feelings*, but these feelings will never again be transformed into emotions relating to a false identity.

There is nothing wrong in placing your awareness in your mind to somehow make sense of the new experiences you have when letting go of emotional limitations and limitations of your sensual capabilities.

For example, if a seemingly blind person suddenly becomes aware that he has eyes and hence, when he opens them he will not be able to make any sense of what he sees. Most likely it will be so blinding that it will just be painful. So he needs to get used to it. He needs his clear mind to find interpretations of what he perceives. Most importantly, he must be willing to expand or change the interpretations again and again so he does not fool himself with false assumptions about his new perceptions.

This is actually how most of the spiritual distractions are born. A person may have a moving and deep intuition or insight; it might even perceive a whole swarm of dragons. Now the question is: What is that person doing with it? Is it using that experience to pump up its esoteric false identity and to impress any new ager he encounters? That way even the deepest experience turns into just another bond chaining that person to its false identity; just another brick in the wall of memories surrounding every false identity.

The wise one just *allows* the experience. The wise one allows the interpretations assigned by his mind to be arbitrarily false. Yet the wise one *knows the truth* about what he felt independently of the form or shape he later assigned to it in order to become more clear about the experience for himself, or in order to convey the experience to others.

As with all metaphors, the blind person metaphor is not really applicable to awakening humans who *rediscover* the greater reality that they have known before they incarnated as humans. That is why your mind should never try to override your knowingness. However, mind and knowingness can eventually make a great team.

I repeat, it is most important not to become attached to any interpretation your mind assigns to a new perception, *because eventually you will let go of any notion anyway!*

See, the subconscious of humanity is filled with notions and concepts related to the greater reality. Humans agreed on these a long time ago when they were more open to other realities.

This is how the notion of "dragon" came into human consciousness. By no means do I look like the dragons depicted in human cultures, but as a human you automatically relate my presence to the shape and attributes of dragons as held in human consciousness.

At some point, humans agreed to illustrate dragons in a certain way. In the west they show us with wings. In the east, without wings. Still both relate to the very same underlying feeling that arises in a dragon's presence. *This is the very way that realities are co-created.*

This understanding of reality, of its notions, forms and interactions, is the key to be a fully sovereign being. The sovereign being understands that *everything is made up*. It can partake in whatever reality for the sake of experience. The sovereign being does not get stuck in any reality because it knows about its own completeness and that it is just visiting a created reality. Still that sovereign being will be in awe and in joy when it discovers or rediscovers all the potentials that creation holds.

My friend, this venturing out into *new realities* as a sovereign being, is actually the dream behind the dream of embodied consciousness. This is what we call the *Third Round of Creation*. And yes, you and the likes of you are the portals into that grandest dream of all. You are paving the way.

I am Althar, the doorkeeper. Nice to see you so close.

10. The End of Being a Limited Human

I am Althar.

Let me finalize the discussion of the emotional body and how to dissolve it. Although your human mind tells you that this is known stuff, first grade psychology, a boring playground for beginners on the way to realization, the dissolving of the emotional body is not an easy task. *Therefore I urge you to follow my explanations.*

The development of the emotional body marks the beginning of the human tragedy of creating false identities, which keeps the human stuck in limitation. It marks the beginning of a journey through many lifetimes where you tried to improve and polish false identities. Among them being a whole range of spiritual identities.

When it dawned on you that none of these identities were *real*, that none of them could ever answer your question "Who am I?" in a lasting satisfying way, you started to surrender, to let go of beliefs and even some false identities.

So over time you have brought more *simplicity* into your emotional body, more clarity, less conflicting parties. With every simplification you felt your life change; you became more in sync with what you really are. People you knew dropped out of your life as they could no longer relate to your simplified emotional body.

The dissolving of the emotional body, *to its completion*, is not for the many. At least not with the current state of human consciousness.

So what to do? I could fondle you for eons to come. I could tell you how wonderful you are being on this journey. What great things you do for yourself and for all of creation. How awesome your insights are. How difficult it is to have an emotional body. Ok, as they are all true statements, I now do it once and for all. Zzzz. Did you feel it? Fine, so let's get real and see why this topic is so delicate.

Dissolving the emotional body is the end of being a limited human!

There is a reason that so few ascended masters walked the earth for a longer period of time. *They left, because staying was too difficult.*

As it is so significant I repeat, *dissolving the emotional body is the end of being a limited human!*

The remaining crystallized emotions are the ones that are *closest to you*. When they speak to you, you hear it as your own voice. Believe me, *true self does not use words!*

Whenever you talk to yourself, *it is the voice of a false identity*. I use the term *false* because that is what they are. False does not mean bad. *They are just not real.* It could be the voice of your version of Mother Theresa wanting to help every one. And most people would applaud you for doing that. Still, false remains false.

When you are in resonance with your own knowingness, *you know*. You might then choose to verbalize it so the mental portion of you can more readily accept what you have come to know. But this is very different from the internal whispering of false identities that just want to sustain and validate themselves.

I already mentioned that the way to dissolve the remaining emotional crystals is to bring pure consciousness into the emotional body. I said that no creation of yours can withstand the presence of your pure consciousness when *you allow it to dissolve.*

However, you will encounter a paradox. When you, as a human, observe yourself in a mirror *you usually do not expect the image in the mirror to vanish.* But the truth is, *it will vanish*; as you have already discovered by yourself. It left you perplexed, shaking your head, *and instantly the image was back.*

The very same will happen when you are centered in your pure consciousness while observing a given emotional crystal. *There is a deep rooted fear of you vanishing.* And the moment you feel the crystal is gone, that fear will come up resulting in you taking on a certain focus – *and back is the crystal.*

Any remaining emotional crystal, like your face in the mirror, is something you have related to throughout your human incarnations.

Are you so courageous to trust that you will still exist even if your face in the mirror vanishes?

Now you might see why I say dissolving the emotional body, the remaining emotional crystals, is the end of being a limited human. It is the end of being stuck in any image of yourself.

Now you might see why so few are so bold as to walk this path to its very end.

Now you know why staying on the planet afterwards is such a challenge.

It is like someone telling you to skin yourself and then to trust that what remains is finally a free and viable being. As drastic as this comparison might sound, it is very accurate from the still limited human's perspective. All the above sounds nice and exciting – until the point where it becomes real and *all unreal vanishes*.

This is the core reason why most humans who went to the very end experienced their full realization at the time of death. Others left their body while letting go of *all* the images they still held of themselves. In that very moment of total surrender, which is still lasting for them, they had the sensation of total integration of what they have ever been. They felt the wholeness within themselves. They felt the bliss of utmost relaxation of their true self and the untarnished clarity about their whole existence. The beauty was overwhelming.

And then, after such an experience, why would they opt to go back into a limited human body and human culture just to be ridiculed, burned at the stake, or nailed to a cross? Only a few did.

I am Althar. I have seen it all. I am a witness of humanity since its very beginning.

Therefore I tell you – *go these last steps slowly, if you want to stay.*

Observing an emotional crystal is not a stare down. It is like the sun just radiating its light, its warmth. If it happens to shine onto an ice cube, that ice cube will just melt, sun does not care.

The moment you *expect* the crystal to disappear while observing it, you fall back into cause and effect. This will never work, it just validates the crystal. Instead, just be in your pure consciousness, in total acceptance. Suddenly the crystal will flicker. Suddenly it is gone. But when you notice that, it will most likely come back, just as your physical image in the mirror came back. *And you just allow that!* At some point the crystals will just vanish, never to come back again. You will be at ease with that – and the two of us will nod our heads and share a smile.

Do not measure your progress! *It is of no importance if it takes a day or decades.* Even if you died today, be assured that you will complete the cycle the moment you leave the physical body. Otherwise, you and the likes of you would not have come this far. Therefore, you have every reason to just relax.

The final remaining crystals you encounter at the end are different from those you encountered at the beginning. Those were weak and feeble. A small exposure to pure consciousness and they were gone. It is like taking off your clothes, which is easy to do because you know the clothes are not you. *But now it is about your skin.*

The fun thing is, the moment you let go of everything, you notice that not even a dragon has skin. Why carry *anything* around? It was all just a creation, rooted in false assumptions about reality and played out by false identities.

And this closes my discussion about the emotional body. Again, I emphasize that dissolving the emotional body is the *only thing of real importance* for you and the likes of you. All the rest that may come through me will essentially be a distraction, comforting you while making this transition.

I am Althar, your personal clarity.

11. The Essence of Energy

I am Althar.

Come. Come with me. It is time to take a journey. A journey to a place you have long forgotten. Feel how the consciousness of the two of us is not separated. Although our respective forms are not connected on a physical level, feel that you can be within my body of consciousness in any intensity and clarity that you choose. While you are doing so, you can remain being fully aware of your physical body, and actually I advise you to do so. Whenever you journey to other realms, with me or on your own, *keep the awareness of your body*.

See, consciousness is a wonderful thing. Humans tend to think they have a given amount of it and if it is split then they have two portions of half of the volume. The truth is, consciousness cannot be measured in terms of size or volume. Consciousness *is*. Consciousness can choose to perceive in as many places at the same time as it wants. Therefore, you can be fully aware in this reality while at the same time travelling with me elsewhere to a single place or multiple places.

I admit though that the human needs to get used to it. Just as it needs to learn how to see and to hear simultaneously, it also needs to learn not to have the various perceptions from this and other realities interfere with each other.

Now come, join me. We are taking off straight into the sun. Ah, the sun. For a dragon the sun is the ultimate relaxation when we have been close to physical reality. Just like everything in physical reality has non-physical layers, so it is with the sun. This is where we go. This is where we *are* already. This is where we take a bath. Note that heat is not an issue for consciousness. Instead, it helps release all tensions that even I, as a dragon, take on when coming so close to you. I guess you can say a sun for a dragon is like a sauna for the human.

Feel the energy of the sun. Make a note of it, as we will refer to it later.

Now let's shake our form while floating inside the sun. I am serious! It helps release all harshness that is so characteristic of physical reality. While doing so, feel your physical body and how it responds. This is another reason for staying aware in your physical body while journeying. Your various parts of consciousness are in resonance with each other, and so is the physical body with the portion of you that is aware of the physical. The moment your consciousness is in delight, your body responds with delight because it resonates with it.

See the earth from the perspective of the sun. So tiny, yet so beautiful. See your human body on that planet, sitting there and grinning while you are out here. Isn't consciousness a wonderful thing?

Let's continue our journey. Turn around! Let the earth be behind you. This is an important symbolic step. You consciously choose to let go of all earthly bonds and limitations. Yes, you remain in resonance with your human portion even while we go beyond the physical reality.

Follow me deeper into the sun. You might see the sun as a portal that leads you out of physicality. However, you do not need such a portal. But why not choose a grand exit with some wonderful light effects if we can?

Where do we go? We will go to a very special place. We have now left the sun and I have chosen us to be in nothingness.

Ah, nothingness. The sun might be great for relaxing after being in physicality, but nothingness is the ultimate for letting go of everything.

Again, take note of your human body. It seems to be far away, right? But did we move at all? Not a bit. No movement at all. Just a portion of our consciousness has shifted. Since you have been a human for so long, and still are, the essence of physicality comes with you. That's why *distance* is a notion that you automatically apply. Now drop that! Let go of the notion of distance.

What if I, Althar, and you and this nothingness sat right on the tip of your human nose? Imagine this for a moment. See, not difficult at all! Consciousness is very flexible once you release it from the physical attributes. You might even imagine additional versions of us being located in your human hands. Just do it. Again, not difficult at all.

Good. Now we leave the human behind and continue our journey. I stated earlier how true self created energy and how I was created using the metaphor of the ocean and the bucket. Let's visit that ocean. How do we do that?

We just feel the *essence of energy*.

This sounds difficult, but it is not. You are aware of the essence of our consciousness, our true self, our "I exist." You are accustomed to going there and then, after a while, jumping directly from there into any reality, most often back into your human reality. Now, instead of making such a big jump, *make the slightest movement you can imagine out of true self*. A tiny, tiny movement, a tiny shift in consciousness.

Remember when you were a kid, having an old fashioned radio and you turned the dial to change the receiving frequency? Sometimes you had to turn the dial very slowly *just before* a more powerful station that was located on the frequency band.

This is very similar to what you are going to do now. Realities that are already created are like powerful radio stations that are highly attractive for you. Their strength overshadow the ring of pure energy that is surrounding your true self, metaphorically speaking – as always. But that ring of pure energy is where we want to go.

Now, allow yourself to do that tiny shift in consciousness out of true self. Relax into it – and suddenly you are there. You are in the midst of an ocean of pure energy, *which is crystallized consciousness of our true self.*

Feel it. This fluid light is true home for any form, any entity ever emitted by your true self.

This energy is you.

This energy will never turn against you!

And this is what I want you to remember. As a human you were permanently in survival mode because every energy on earth can turn against you at any moment! The sun might feel warm on your skin, but expose your skin for too long and it will burn you. The ocean looks lovely and fresh, but a large wave could crush you on the shore.

Now you might grasp why entities who have never walked the earth cannot imagine what a human is going through. Amongst all entities in all of existence, only the humans have completely forgotten where they came from.

Dwell in this energy for this is your home.

Dwell in this energy and know – *it will never turn against you.* Feel it.

Take your time.

*

Feel your human on earth! That portion of consciousness now *knows* just as the portion that is here *knows*.

Feel your biology. It relaxes. Why? Because your human consciousness has let go of the grip and demands of the body. The body doesn't fear death. It is in constant change anyway. It is just fine with physical energies as they are; it is made out of them. *It was the false identities held by your emotional body that were in fear of eradication and therefore dominated the physical body.*

Recall the energy of the sun. It felt good and relaxing, didn't it? But there is simply no comparison to this energy of home.

My dear friend, I will leave you now, for this is your moment.

Once again, you need to make a choice. Leave the human reality or keep some portion of you in that reality. This is up to you.

Know this: There is no obligation of any kind.

Also know, you can come back here any time. Any time.

I am Althar, the Crystal Dragon, it is a delight to see you in delight.

12. The Family of Uriel

I am Althar.

Let's speak about our spiritual family, the family of Uriel. As you know, the entities once gathered into groups, much like humans gather into groups. Together it was easier to face existence, to go through experiences and to ponder – or avoid – the question of "Who am I?"

Just like groups of humans, other entities find a certain stability and convenience when they can take on and even identify with a set of beliefs. It is like standing with your peers in a circle and everybody is backslapping its neighbors. It feels quite good. At least this gathering and gesture validates that you are not alone with your beliefs, therefore you cannot be that wrong.

This mechanism has been in place up to now *in all realms of existence*. Even the associated group dynamics are similar throughout the cosmos.

The family of Uriel is known to be *as close to source as possible*.

Remember what I said about my dragon nature? It is as close to true self as possible, yet it is individualized.

I will now try to convey something, which you cannot understand with your human mind. The human mind is bound to cause and effect. It can only see sequences and progressions. It wants one state of being to result from the previous state of being. Well, this is far from the way things are. But for the sake of making my point clear, I will twist the underlying principles into a concept that the mind can somehow accept.

Consider your human body. It consists of atoms, which consists of a nucleus and electrons circling around it. According to your current physics these electrons are quite fast. In fact, *unbelievably fast*. You take that for granted. You assume they will continue their frantic movement in the next moment. Your human consciousness doesn't care a bit about the underlying physics and constantly moves that body without the slightest clue how it achieves this.

My point is, a portion of true self's consciousness *accepts a given setup and starts experiencing within it, not caring for the details!*

When beings came into existence, things happened simultaneously. A human mind would call it extremely fast, but actually it was beyond time. You might say events changed the preceding events resulting in a more refined version of themselves. Thus, beliefs emerged, energies were created and structures composed. Consciousness went outside itself and *started experiencing in these structures, not caring for the details.*

This is the way of the creator, you see. *The details do take care of themselves.*

Suddenly, there were beings outside their respective true selves. They started experiencing according to the very underlying structures *they accepted as their platform of existence.* They created identities around their experiences. And many of those beings still stick to the very first identities they have ever created.

The family of Uriel is a loose association of beings that remained very clear about their respective true selves. Wherever they went, whatever emanations they sent out, they went there with the innate knowingness that *all realities are but creations.* That is why the Uriel family is also known as *the bearers of light,* which would better be stated as *the bearers of pure consciousness.*

An entity of the Uriel family is extremely curious to observe the ways of creation and to discover the most basic design principles that allow creation in the first place. By doing so, such an entity is an adventurer and scientist at the same time. Such an entity is *intense.* It always seeks to cut away false notions and false interpretations. It is always ready to redefine itself. It does not rest until once again it stands in the midst of a given reality and *undoubtedly, embraces both its true self and that reality.*

In your earthly reality, humans of the family of Uriel are loved and feared at the same time. They are loved because they radiate a certain clarity that can easily be felt. They are feared, because that clarity exposes the false identities of others.

This is why the dragon is mostly depicted as being aggressive. It needs to be slain by the knight to earn the affection of the princess or to reclaim the treasure the dragon protects. It is the false identities of the knight that requires slaying. And whoever comes close to a dragon, or an entity of the Uriel family, should be aware of that. Once the false identity is disenchanted, true love awaits the being that was so bold to face the dragon. A lasting love from true self. The treasure that has been within all the time becomes available again.

There is one more thing that needs to be mentioned when it comes to the family of Uriel. As a group, those entities were among the first who discovered, and to a degree, experienced the *principle of ascension*. They came to accept their true selves as full creator beings beyond the question of "Who am I?" Then they went out and tried to make other entities aware of that – but usually they failed.

When it came to create the consensus reality *earth*, an effort commonly undertaken by all of the angelic families, the family of Uriel was one of the driving forces. Not only because of its "engineering" capabilities it has achieved by studying the principles of creation, but more so because it saw the potential for many to realize ascension when things unfold in extreme slow motion. The members of Uriel were actually thrilled by the concept, and you might say, they were very active in recruiting other entities to dive into that adventure.

My dear friend, recently you discovered that having recruited other entities became a burden for you and the likes of you, and it served as a reason to procrastinate ascension.

The ways of the humans have been and are quite brutal in many ways, and many beings have been stuck in this reality for a long time. In a sense you might say, the idea of earth was brilliant, but the design had some flaws. So you, and the likes of you, felt a certain guilt for having apparently made false promises. And even though you could have left many lifetimes ago, you kept on coming back, and coming back, and coming back. You tried to fix something that you considered to be flawed. You tried to diminish the feelings of guilt by attempting to teach others about pure consciousness so they could free themselves.

You know – *let go of this!* This is just another false identity! A noble one, you might say, but very worn out by now and fuddy-duddy. Even though you claim for yourself that you have already released that, well, it still sticks here and there a little bit, and isn't that getting boring?

We have learned from the earth experience. New earths are built. Enhanced versions you might say. The beings that are on your earth are just fine. Even though they might be stuck, they are in experiences that they will cherish into eternity.

For you my friend, it is time to embrace the earthly reality *as it is*. Be at peace with it. *Enjoy it while you are still around.*

I will be with you to remind you. The moment you feel that fiery breath on your neck, it is me, Althar, reminding you of who you really are.

I will be nudging you to energetically turn around in your human body, to face me, to face your true self, and *to let go of all earthly concerns*. Details do take care of themselves.

I am Althar, a bearer of pure consciousness.

13. The Principle of Ascension

I am Althar.

Let me expand more on the family of Uriel by first telling you that the role the families played is coming to an end. Why? Because once an entity comes to full realization, it goes beyond its family.

I said the entities comprising that family are loosely connected. They are loosely connected for they do *not* share a common set of beliefs, but rather the same knowingness of their respective true self. Therefore they honor each other, they enjoy gathering and exchanging, but *they do not need each other* to validate their existence.

When I speak about characteristics of the Uriel family, it does not mean that these are exclusive to that family. Of course, other families share these traits and explore them, usually though in conjunction with other primary interests. In other words, the entities of Uriel found themselves being almost exclusively attracted to uncover the ways of pure consciousness. They were not that attracted to or, as some might say, distracted by the wealth of other potentials.

I also said that the entities of the family of Uriel were among the first who discovered the principle of ascension and I want to clarify this to some extent. Again, this will be quite difficult to grasp from the perspective of human consciousness. Nevertheless, I will try.

Everything outside true self is but a creation. Moreover, creation in the non-physical realms is *instant*. Therefore, it is hard to separate the initial intent from the result. Also a change in the intent immediately changes what has been created. To simplify things one could say non-physical creation is quite fluid and even fuzzy. This is why it is so difficult for a human to place its awareness out there and to perceive anything meaningful for the human mind. Things seem to constantly change. And they do!

Now imagine an entity in the other realms pondering the question "Who am I?" Imagine this entity suddenly having a revelation, an insight into the nature of its true self. Since everything out there is kind of fleeting and fuzzy, *so is that very realization of true self.* Consequently, there remains a certain doubt about the validity of the insight. Is it just another creation? A nice concept? As authentic as the original insight might have been, that entity carries a certain amount of doubt about that very insight.

That's why I call it *the principle of ascension* when it occurs in the other realms. It is close to real ascension. So close, but not quite firm – a residue of doubt remains.

Contrary to the non-physical realms, the physical reality appears to be so very solid. So extremely slow. So cause and effect. It is equally just a creation, *but to the human it appears to be real.* Real in such a rigid sense that many fight for it to be the only reality.

The good thing about this setup is that any true insight you gain while being in this solid, harsh, slow motion reality *has enormous validity for your true self!*

As strange as that might sound to you, true self suddenly *knows* that its former intuition of ascension actually *is real,* for you are the living proof!

You had forgotten all about yourself, just as true self did when it became aware of its own existence – and *you came to the very same insight.* Despite all difficulties. Despite all pain. Despite all distractions.

*

Dear friend, let's shift gears now.

I am Althar, the Crystal Dragon.

There were times on earth when humans were more aware of us. Some had dragon aspects of themselves and they knew it. Others felt the presence of dragons as Ambassadors of Creation.

Over time humans stopped perceiving dragons. You might say they had forgotten. You might say they had closed their greater awareness. You might also say that the dragons had retracted a bit. And all of the above is true.

But now, I declare – *the dragons are coming back. Not just a few, but in legions.*

We will make ourselves perceivable to those

who are open and courageous enough to be in the presence of pure consciousness. We do not come to interfere, but to serve as *catalysts*.

Therefore, I ask you, dear friend, consider releasing these messages to a broader audience. You have learned that the acceptance of dragons into your greater reality, or even acknowledging a dragon aspect as part of yourself, requires a certain leap in consciousness. Knowing other people who share the same experiences can be of great help.

I am Althar, the elder.

14. More on Dragons and Crystal Dragons

I am Althar.

So you want more clarity about the nature of dragons and specifically about the crystal dragons.

When I introduced myself I said dragons are guides. Although I used the term "guide," the guiding we do is very different from what the new agers call angel guides.

You and I emanated from the same true self, so in a certain sense you can say we are one entity. Still we are quite different in so many ways. For an analogy consider your human body. Your eyes and your stomach belong to your body, they share the same DNA, and still they have completely different ways of functioning, experiencing and interpreting their respective environments. Because their experiences are so different it would be very hard for your stomach to translate insights of the eyes into "stomach language" or vice versa. Thanks to a good design though, there is no need for them to do this. They operate on a shared basis of knowingness, each in its own realm, but mutually aware of the other body parts.

The relation between you and me is somewhat similar. I, representing the eyes, have the advantage of having an overview by seeing. I can perceive our common body in its entirety whereas you, representing the stomach, have the advantage of a deep physical experience. You are shielded from so many outside influences, which allow you to keenly focus on the aspects of your environment that remain within your sensual awareness.

So what do dragons guide? *Dragons guide energies*.

Dragons help to prepare and sustain the stages of creation in a certain structure so that other entities *can experience within them*.

Consider a kaleidoscope. What a great invention! Take a few mirrors facing each other at certain angles, add some colored shards into the space between those mirrors and the results are stunningly beautiful formations. Assume you were such a colored shard and you dove into this arrangement of mirrors with some of your good and even not-so-good friends. Each shard can move independently, constantly giving rise to new arrangements. In addition, the mirrors rotate all by themselves, so that settings are constantly changing. Sounds amazing, doesn't it? Can you see the beauty in the *simplicity of the design* that allows the creation of an infinite number of beautiful arrangements, expressions and experiences? This is where dragons get thrilled.

The setup of earth is quite similar to that of a kaleidoscope, albeit much more refined. It requires many different mirrors on many energetic levels. The role of dragons is to manifest the mirrors, to keep them in shape and to keep them moving. This is a way of describing how *dragons guide energies*.

As a result of this, the eastern cultures on earth, in particular, are aware of so many nature bound dragons. They not only associate dragons with the basic elements such as fire or water, but also with rivers, mountains and trees. And rightfully so.

So this is the primary role of dragons, not only for earth, but for all realities.

Now assume you were a mirror in a kaleidoscope. This is a completely different role and perspective from that of a shard. *Now you are aware of the underlying design itself.* You observe how those shards explore their reality in amazement. That way you get a lot of clarity about the reality created by the kaleidoscope. For example, what behavior it induces and what understandings it allows. However, serving as a mirror is a very different experience compared with that of a given shard that is *living the experiences.*

This is why I, Althar, as well as the other dragons coming in, are not here to teach or to interfere. We come in to provide a greater clarity for those who ask for it, for those who are ready to *let go of their limited existence as a colored shard.* Being a shard is interesting for a while, but eventually coming back to wholeness is why the shard took on that disguise in the first place.

Dragons also evolve. They change roles over time. They gain wisdom by being in service as a guide for various energies and observing the experiences other entities have while playing in those energies. They gain understanding of energy designs and they gain understanding of the ways of consciousness.

Not all humans have a dragon self and not all dragons have a human self. Given a mutual interest, a human can bond with any dragon. However, whenever a dragon *melds* with a human it generally means that the human and the dragon emanated from the same true self. Moreover, it means that *both* are ready for that experience. They both let go of the blocking filters they have used to shield their respective consciousness. Additionally, the dragon lets go of its role of being in service as an energy guide.

As exciting as such an experience is for the human, it is just as exciting for the dragon! For not only can the human now see through the dragon's eyes, *it is also the dragon that can see through the human's eyes!* It is a two-way gift that the human and the dragon provide each other. Call it a love affair that is destined to have a happy ending.

Of course dragons continue evolving even after they have melded with an incarnated human self. If that human disincarnates, the dragon continues its dragon existence enriched by the wisdom it has gained while being so close with the human.

There were times when humans and dragons were closer and the bonding, or even melding, of humans and dragons was not unusual. A dragon that has ripened and gained wisdom through a number of meldings or bondings with humans, or its human selves, is called a crystal dragon.

Note that there is no hierarchy of any sort amongst the dragons. A crystal dragon is no better than a dragon of fire. We do not rate a diamond higher than coal. Actually we do not rate at all; we just marvel at the enormous variety of possible creations. And we do know that any diamond returns to coal if it is exposed to sufficiently strong heat.

Still, by their very nature, dragons are in awe of wisdom. Therefore, they naturally honor those who have already had many experiences. This is true for dragons amongst themselves, and it is specifically true with respect to humans.

I am Althar, a crystal in the beautiful kaleidoscope of creation.

15. The Third Round of Creation

I am Althar.

So you ask about the Third Round of Creation.

This phrase is primarily being used by the family of Uriel amongst each other. The first round of creation was the original consciousness. It just *was*. It suddenly felt its own existence and asked, "Who am I?" Thus, it burst forth. In a sense you might say it has split itself into individualized fragments of itself. We call each of these fragments *true self.* Pure consciousness beyond identity, yet individualized and sovereign.

This split was *final.* There is no way the fragments could ever reunite and reestablish the original consciousness. It is the same with the pollen of a flower, which will never reunite with the flower it came from. Nevertheless, there is the remembrance of that initial oneness and even a longing to go back. Call it the original trauma accompanying the sudden realization "I exist."

If a cell of your body is stripped from the body, it will die. It has lost its greater being and has no way to survive on its own. A cell needs energy to sustain itself. It needs energy coming from the outside, which is then transformed by all of the body so the cell and the whole body can continue to live.

Consciousness, however, just *is*. It does not need energy from the outside to sustain its beingness. Therefore, these initial true selves *just continued existing*. Even if they wanted to die, to lose their existence because of that total absence of the initial oneness, *they couldn't!* They continued to *be*. They continued to be in a total void. Nothing. Humans speak of birth trauma. Actually, the human birth trauma is by design; it is used to mimic this initial feeling of loss of the true self. You see, at its very core, *things are always simple.*

Note that this initial fragmentation is very different from the way your true self emanates entities or representations of itself. Whatever it has emitted *has the potential of reuniting.* Every human could go on and on from incarnation to incarnation, never coming back to its true self. This is the freedom of the human. However, the moment a human chooses to reunite with its true self *it can do so.* It might take a while though, even lifetimes, but in the end it will work out.

So, what we refer to as the Second Round of Creation is the true selves exploring their creator abilities, yet with the underlying question "Who am I?" in conjunction with an ingrained doubt about the very validity of their existence *outside the initial one.* We call this *the wound of creation.*

When a human realizes its own true self – without any doubt, not just as a concept, but as a living experience – and finally stops questioning itself and comes to the realization *"I am that I am,"* then that human ends the search as well as the self-doubt *on behalf of its entire true self.*

Finally, true self has accepted itself in its totality. Finally, true self ceases to play any energy games whatsoever. Finally, true self *embraces its own creatorship*. Finally, true self is free to create without agenda *as no false identity or search for identity or self-doubt distorts its creations!*

See, without that final acceptance, every creation somehow carries the question "Who am I?" It is distorted by this nagging uncertainty and this longing for completeness. Even the pure energy created by true self has that taste!

Now that the search is over, now that the doubt is released, *even that pure energy of true self changes*. It reflects the acceptance that true self has gained of itself as a full creator being. You might now call it *new energy*.

Dear friend, can you feel the dream that underlies ascension?

Ascension gives rise to undistorted creation!

This is what we call the Third Round of Creation. Feel it. Just feel it and pause for a moment.

*

There is an open question, which is specifically interesting in relation to your earth reality: Can undistorted creation co-exist with the purpose-driven creation of the second round?

Nobody knows yet. This is why you and the likes of you have decided to embody the highest consciousness possible on earth *as long as you can stand it.* This is partly because of the residue of wanting to help others and partly because you came to love earth, nature, and even humanity so much that it is hard for you to leave. *But mostly you want to stay because it is such a great adventure.*

Essentially, an ascended being has the option to just do what the initial consciousness has done: to burst forth into existence; to give birth to individualized portions of itself and to grant them total freedom with no way back. However, this time these portions will not carry that question of "Who am I?" They will *know* what they are right from the beginning and will not even be burdened with the history of experiences that led to that final realization. Thus, they will be utterly *fresh.*

The Third Round of Creation means *undistorted creation.* No underlying question to answer, no doubt to erase; just *creation for the sake of creation.*

Can you feel the excitement that comes with it? Can you see the *grandness of consciousness?* No matter how exhausting, boring, or painful your personal current situation on planet earth is, get in resonance with this greater picture and feel the relief and joy it will bring to you.

Stay on earth or leave, as you wish. No matter what you choose – existence will enter the Third Round of Creation. It can do so only because of the way of humans; thanks to your way of being, dear reader.

I am Althar, an Ambassador of Creation, in honor of the way of humans.

16. A Note from True Self

I am Aouwa.
I am your source.
I am still.
I know who I am.
I am free.

I have dropped any need to mirror myself to me.
I create for the joy of creating.

I will ever go beyond, for that is my nature.

Do dragons exist?
Do humans exist?
Do dreams exist?

I am Althar.
Althar is an emanation of me.
I am you.
You are an emanation of me.
Whatever I dream into life becomes life.

You, human, have a choice.

You heard it all.
Heard it through so many voices.
Heard it in so many expressions.
Heard it through Althar.
Heard it in your own heart.

Dear friend,
I invite you.
I invite you to relax into me.
I invite you to experience the unlimited.
I invite you to be at ease with self.
I invite you to embody this unlimited potential.
The potential to create without distortion.
The choice is yours.

You ask what to do in your human life?
Do not think as a human.
Do not feel as a human.
Instead, be in resonance with me.
Every moment.
Come to me.
I am here.
I have always been here.
I am you.

When being in resonance with me,
receive the moment.
Each moment.
Just receive.
This will let you see yourself
In all that is.

Then you may join me in saying:
I am creation. Therefore I am free!

*

Acknowledgements

I would like to express my heartfelt gratitude to Charmaine Wagner for her encouragement during the creation process and support in editing the manuscript. Thanks, Charmaine!

Made in the USA
Las Vegas, NV
19 March 2021